The Open Road Awaits:

Plan, Pack And Prepare For Your Best Trip Ever

INTRODUCTION

Welcome, fellow traveler, to the gateway of adventure! In the following pages, we are set to embark on a journey that transcends the ordinary, where the open road becomes a canvas for the extraordinary. This eBook is your compass, your guide, and your confidante as you navigate the realms of trip planning, packing strategies, and thorough preparation – all with the singular goal of ensuring that your upcoming adventure is nothing short of your best trip ever.

Begin your journey by delving into the allure of the open road. What is it about the idea of a journey that captures our imagination and fuels our desire for exploration? In this chapter, we explore the psychology behind travel, the innate human longing for discovery, and how embracing the call of the open road can be a transformative experience.

Crafting Your Dream Itinerary

A great trip starts with a great plan. Learn the art of crafting a dream itinerary that aligns with your travel goals, interests, and time constraints. We'll delve into the factors to consider when choosing your destination, the magic of off-the-beaten-path exploration, and how to strike the right balance between planned activities and spontaneous adventures.

Not all who wander are lost, but a little guidance in destination selection can go a long way. This chapter is your compass in choosing the perfect locale for your adventure. Explore tips on researching destinations, understanding your travel preferences, and discovering hidden gems that may be just off the map but well worth the detour.

The Art of Efficient Packing

Packing can be an art form, and this is your palette. From mastering the art of minimalist packing to ensuring you have all the essentials for your journey, we'll cover the dos and don'ts of packing. Dive into strategies for organizing your belongings, making the most of limited space, and incorporating. the latest travel gear and gadgets into your repertoire.

Navigating Travel Logistics

A smooth journey relies on solid logistics. From booking flights to arranging transportation at your destination, this chapter provides a comprehensive guide to navigating the logistical maze of travel. Uncover tips on finding the best deals, understanding travel insurance, and ensuring a seamless transition from home to your chosen destination.

Life on the road is inherently unpredictable, but fear not – preparation is the key to overcoming the unexpected. Explore strategies for managing travel emergencies, staying healthy on the road, and handling unforeseen challenges with grace. Equip yourself with the knowledge and tools to transform potential obstacles into opportunities for growth and adventure.

Immersing Yourself in Local Culture

Travel is not just about the places you go; it's about the people you meet and the cultures you encounter. This chapter is a guide to immersing yourself in the local culture, fostering meaningful connections, and embracing the richness of diversity. Learn how to respectfully engage with locals, savor authentic culinary experiences, and contribute positively to the communities you visit.

Capturing Moments, Creating Memories

A trip is not truly complete without a collection of cherished memories. In this chapter, we explore the art of capturing moments through photography, journaling, and other creative means. Discover how to document your journey in a way that not only preserves the memories for yourself but also inspires others to embark on their adventures.

Post-Trip Reflection and Integration

As your journey concludes, the adventure doesn't end – it transforms into a reservoir of experiences that can shape your perspective for years to come. This final chapter guides you through the process of post-trip reflection and integration. Explore ways to carry the lessons and insights from your travels into your daily life, fostering a continued sense of adventure and curiosity.

CHAPTER 1-THE BENEFITS OF TRAVEL

A Tapestry of Human Experiences

From the moment our ancestors first set foot on the shores of new lands, an innate curiosity has driven us to explore the vast expanse of our planet. This insatiable desire to venture beyond the familiar, to push the boundaries of our comfort zones, and to discover the wonders that lie beyond our immediate surroundings is a testament to the profound allure of travel. It is a force that has shaped civilizations, connected cultures, and enriched our understanding of the world and ourselves.

Throughout history, the human spirit of exploration has propelled us across continents and oceans, leading to the discovery of new lands, the expansion of trade routes, and the dissemination of knowledge and ideas. From the intrepid Phoenician sailors who navigated the Mediterranean Sea to the courageous explorers who ventured into the uncharted territories of the Americas and beyond, our thirst for the unknown has been a driving force behind some of humanity's greatest achievements.

The allure of travel is not merely a modern phenomenon. It has captivated imaginations since the dawn of human civilization. Ancient mariners braved treacherous seas to reach distant shores, driven by the promise of trade, adventure, and the discovery of new lands. Land explorers, fueled by curiosity and ambition, ventured into uncharted territories, mapping the contours of continents, documenting the diversity of life, and forging connections with diverse cultures.

The legacy of exploration is not confined to the past. In today's interconnected world, travel has become more accessible than ever before. With a multitude of destinations and modes of transportation available, the world is our oyster. Yet, despite the ease of travel, the allure of the unfamiliar remains as strong as ever. We are still drawn to the exotic, the mysterious, and the untamed, yearning to experience cultures and landscapes that lie beyond our borders.

Travel is more than just a leisure activity; it is a transformative experience that can shape our perspectives, enrich our lives, and leave an indelible mark on our souls. Through travel, we gain a deeper understanding of the world and our place in it. We learn to appreciate the diversity of human experience, the richness of different cultures, and the beauty of the natural world. We also develop a greater sense of empathy, compassion, and tolerance, as we come into contact with people from different backgrounds and walks of life.

Travel is a catalyst for personal growth, pushing us beyond our comfort zones and forcing us to confront our fears and insecurities. It is in these moments of vulnerability that we truly discover ourselves, uncovering hidden talents, cultivating self-awareness, and emerging from our journeys with a renewed sense of purpose and direction.

So, what are you waiting for? Embark on a journey of exploration, venture beyond your comfort zone, and discover the wonders that await you. The world is a vast and fascinating place, filled with endless possibilities for adventure and self-discovery. Let the allure of travel guide you, and embark on a journey that will transform you forever. As you embark on your travels, remember that the true essence of exploration lies not just in reaching new destinations but in the transformative experiences that unfold along the way. Embrace the unexpected, immerse yourself in the local cultures, and allow yourself to be transformed by the wonders that lie beyond your familiar shores.

Travel, in its myriad forms, serves as a gateway to a world of endless possibilities, shattering the confines of our familiar surroundings and introducing us to a kaleidoscope of cultures, traditions, and landscapes. As we journey through bustling cities, serene country sides, and ancient ruins, we encounter a tapestry of human experiences, each with its unique rhythm, flavor, and beauty.

Immersion in diverse cultures broadens our perspectives, challenging our preconceived notions and fostering empathy. We learn to appreciate the nuances of different lifestyles, the rich heritage that shapes each society, and the common threads that bind us together as a global community. We discover that amidst the diversity of human expression, there lies a shared humanity that connects us all.

Travel is not merely about observing; it is about engaging, interacting, and immersing ourselves in the heart of different cultures. It is about savoring the flavors of authentic cuisine, participating in local festivals, and engaging in meaningful conversations with people from all walks of life. Through these interactions, we gain a deeper understanding of the world, not from textbooks or news reports, but from the firsthand experiences of those who live it.

Embracing the Tapestry of Human Cultures

Travel is a passport to a kaleidoscope of cultures, each with its unique traditions, beliefs, and customs. Immersing ourselves in these diverse environments fosters empathy, appreciation, and a profound sense of interconnectedness. We witness the resilience of human spirit, the ingenuity of diverse traditions, and the beauty of shared humanity. In our world, a vibrant tapestry of cultures is woven together, each with its unique threads of traditions, beliefs, and customs. Embracing this tapestry is akin to embarking on a journey of endless discovery, where we broaden our horizons, deepen our understanding, and forge meaningful connections with humanity's diverse tapestry.

Across the globe, cultures have evolved over time, preserving and passing down their unique traditions. These traditions, from the vibrant Holi celebrations in India to the solemn tea ceremonies in Japan, provide a glimpse into the heart of each culture, offering insights into their values, beliefs, and ways of life.

Personal Growth and Self-Discovery: A Journey Within

Travel is not merely a journey through foreign lands; it is a voyage of self-discovery. Far from the comforts of home, we confront our limitations, adapt to new environments, and uncover hidden strengths within ourselves. Navigating unfamiliar territories demands resourcefulness, adaptability, and resilience.

We step outside our routines, embrace spontaneity, and develop a newfound appreciation for the simple joys of life.

Through the challenges and triumphs we encounter, we gain a deeper understanding of our values, passions, and aspirations. We discover that we are capable of far more than we ever imagined, possessing a reservoir of inner strength and resilience that lies dormant until we are called upon to adapt and overcome.

Travel is a catalyst for personal growth, pushing us beyond our comfort zones and forcing us to confront our fears and insecurities. It is in these moments of vulnerability that we truly discover ourselves, uncovering hidden talents, cultivating self-awareness, and emerging from our journeys with a renewed sense of purpose and direction.

Enhancing Creativity and Problem-Solving Skills: A Tapestry of New Perspectives

Immersion in diverse environments and exposure to new perspectives stimulate our creativity and enhance our problem-solving abilities. By observing different ways of life, we challenge our assumptions and develop a more flexible approach to thinking. We learn to see the world through different lenses, to question our own ingrained patterns of thought, and to embrace the unconventional.

As we navigate complex situations in unfamiliar settings, we learn to adapt our strategies, draw on our resourcefulness, and find innovative solutions. We develop a mindset of openness and adaptability, embracing challenges as opportunities for growth and learning.

Travel is a training ground for creative thinking and problem-solving, exposing us to a diverse range of perspectives and approaches. It teaches us to think outside the box, to break free from conventional thinking patterns, and to find new and creative solutions to the challenges we encounter.

Promoting Health and Well-being: A Respite for the Mind and Body

Travel has a profound impact on our overall health and well-being. It provides a much-needed respite from the daily stresses of work and routine, allowing us to relax, recharge, and reconnect with ourselves.

Immersion in nature's beauty, engagement in physical activities, and exposure to diverse cultures have a restorative effect on our minds and bodies. We return from our travels feeling refreshed, energized, and better equipped to tackle the demands of daily life.

Travel is an antidote to the stress and burnout that can accumulate in our modern lifestyles. It provides us with an opportunity to disconnect from the constant demands of technology, to step away from the pressures of work and responsibilities, and to focus on our own well-being.

Strengthening Relationships and Building Memories: Bonds That Last a Lifetime

Travel provides a unique platform for strengthening bonds with loved ones and creating lasting memories. Sharing new experiences, navigating unfamiliar territory, and overcoming challenges together forge deeper connections and foster a sense of camaraderie.

As we explore new destinations, we document our journeys through photographs, souvenirs, and stories that we cherish for years to come. These tangible reminders of our adventures become treasured keepsakes, evoking fond memories and rekindling the spirit of exploration.

CHAPTER 2

MAKING THE MOST OF YOUR TRIP

Travel is an adventure that opens our minds, broadens our horizons, and creates memories that last a lifetime. It's an opportunity to step outside of our comfort zones, embrace the unexpected, and connect with people and places from all corners of the globe. Whether you're exploring bustling cities, immersing yourself in serene nature, or embarking on an adventurous trek, travel offers something for everyone.

To truly make the most of your trip, it's essential to approach it with a sense of planning, flexibility, and an open mind. This comprehensive guide will equip you with the knowledge and strategies to transform your next journey into an unforgettable experience.

Define Your Goals and Interests

Before setting off on your travels, take some time to reflect on what you hope to gain from your experience. What are your passions, interests, and curiosities? Are you seeking cultural immersion, historical exploration, breathtaking natural wonders, or exhilarating adventures? Understanding your motivations will help you tailor your itinerary and choose destinations that align with your interests.

Research Your Destination

Once you've identified your goals, delve into researching your chosen destination. Immerse yourself in the local culture, customs, and etiquette. Learn about the language, currency, and essential phrases that will aid in your interactions with locals. Research the must- see attractions, hidden gems, and off-the-beaten-path experiences that align with your interests.

While having a plan is crucial, it's equally important to maintain flexibility. Allow room for spontaneous discoveries, unexpected encounters, and changes in circumstances. Don't be afraid to veer off the beaten path and explore at your own pace.

Pack Light and Smart

Resist the urge to over pack. Pack light and strategically, considering the climate, activities, and duration of your trip. Choose versatile clothing that can be easily mixed and matched, and prioritize comfort over style. Pack essentials like toiletries, medications, and travel documents.

Arrange Accommodations

Research and book accommodations that suit your style and budget. Consider your desired location, amenities, and proximity to attractions. Read reviews from previous guests to get insights into the property and its service.

Even basic phrases in the local language can go a long way in enhancing your travel experience. It demonstrates respect for the culture and can help you communicate with locals, ask for directions, and navigate everyday situations.

Arrange Transportation and Insurance

Research and book transportation options, whether it's flights, trains, buses, or rental cars. Consider the cost, convenience, and duration of each mode of transport. Purchase travel insurance to protect yourself against unforeseen circumstances, such as medical emergencies, flight cancellations, or lost luggage.

Be Present and Immerse Yourself

Put away your phone, resist the urge to constantly check social media, and fully immerse yourself in the present moment. Engage with your surroundings, soak in the sights, sounds, and smells, and savor the unique atmosphere of each destination.

Travel is an opportunity to push your boundaries and try new things. Embrace activities that step outside your comfort zone, whether it's trying local cuisine, engaging in unfamiliar customs, or participating in adventurous activities.

Connect with Locals

Strike up conversations with locals, ask for recommendations, and learn about their perspectives and experiences. Embrace their hospitality and willingness to share their culture. Respect local customs, dress appropriately, and be mindful of religious practices and social norms. Show appreciation for the cultural heritage and traditions of the places you visit.

Be open to unexpected encounters, unplanned detours, and unforeseen circumstances. These spontaneous moments can often lead to the most memorable and enriching experiences of your trip.

Stay Safe and Informed

Familiarize yourself with the safety precautions and advisories for your destination. Be aware of local scams, common tourist traps, and potential risks. Stay informed about local news and weather updates.

Research the climate of your destination and pack accordingly. Pack layers for fluctuating temperatures, appropriate footwear for various activities, and essentials like rain gear or sun protection.

TRAVEL TIPS FOR FISRT TIMERS

The thrill of embarking on your first adventure can be both exhilarating and daunting. Stepping into the unknown, immersing yourself in new cultures, and navigating unfamiliar territories can be a whirlwind of experiences. But with careful planning, an open mind, and a sense of adventure, your first travel experience can be truly transformative.

The allure of travel is undeniable, beckoning us to explore the world's diverse landscapes, immerse ourselves in rich cultures, and forge unforgettable memories. For first-time travelers, embarking on this journey can be both exhilarating and daunting. The prospect of navigating unfamiliar territories, interacting with new people, and adapting to different customs can be overwhelming. However, with careful planning, an open mind, and a sense of adventure, your first travel experience can be truly transformative.

This comprehensive guide is designed to equip first- time travelers with the knowledge and strategies to make the most of their adventures. From planning and preparation to embracing the unexpected, this guide will empower you to confidently navigate the world and create lasting memories.

Define Your Travel Goals and Interests

Before diving into the specifics of your trip, take some time to reflect on your travel aspirations. What are your passions, curiosities, and desires? Do you seek cultural immersion, historical exploration, breathtaking natural wonders, or exhilarating adventures? Understanding your motivations will help you tailor your itinerary and choose destinations that align with your interests.

Travel is a tapestry of experiences, woven from threads of diverse cultures, breathtaking landscapes, and enriching encounters. To truly embark on a meaningful journey, it's essential to define your travel goals and interests, allowing you to curate an itinerary that resonates with your passions and aspirations.

Before setting off on your adventure, take some time for introspection. What ignites your curiosity? What kind of experiences do you crave? Are you drawn to the vibrant tapestry of urban life, the serenity of untouched nature, or the allure of historical landmarks?

Consider your passions, whether it's the pulsating rhythm of music, the culinary artistry of different cuisines, or the captivating tales of ancient civilizations. Let your dreams guide you, envisioning yourself immersed in environments that stir your soul.

The world offers a kaleidoscope of experiences, catering to diverse interests and preferences. Delve into the realm of cultural immersion, where you can engage with local communities, learn traditional practices, and savor authentic cuisine.

Embrace the thrill of adventure by embarking on hikes through rugged terrains, kayaking through pristine waters, or exploring uncharted territories. If relaxation is your quest, seek out tranquil retreats, rejuvenating spa treatments, and serene natural escapes.

Your travel goals should be as unique as you are. Don't feel confined by conventional travel trends or societal expectations. Allow your individuality to shine through, crafting an itinerary that reflects your passions and desires.

Whether it's immersing yourself in the vibrant arts scene of a European metropolis, embarking on a wildlife safari through the African savanna, or exploring the ancient temples of Southeast Asia, let your heart guide you towards experiences that ignite your soul.

Create a Flexible Itinerary

Striking a Balance between Planning and Spontaneity. While having a plan is crucial, it's equally important to maintain flexibility. Allow room for spontaneous discoveries, unexpected encounters, and changes in circumstances. Don't be afraid to veer off the beaten path and explore at your own pace.

CHAPTER 2- CHOOSE YOUR DESTINATION

The allure of travel is undeniable, beckoning us to explore the world's diverse landscapes, immerse ourselves in rich cultures, and forge unforgettable memories. With countless destinations to choose from, each offering its own unique blend of experiences, deciding where to embark on your next adventure can be a daunting task.

However, by taking the time to reflect on your personal aspirations, travel style, and interests, you can narrow down your options and identify the perfect destination that aligns with your dreams.

A Tapestry of Possibilities

The world offers a kaleidoscope of experiences, catering to diverse interests and preferences. Delve into the realm of cultural immersion, where you can engage with local communities, learn traditional practices, and savor authentic cuisine.

Embrace the thrill of adventure by embarking on hikes through rugged terrains, kayaking through pristine waters, or exploring uncharted territories. If relaxation is your quest, seek out tranquil retreats, rejuvenating spa treatments, and serene natural escapes.

Are you a spontaneous adventurer, eager to embrace the unexpected, or do you prefer a well-structured itinerary? Do you crave the vibrant energy of bustling cityscapes or the tranquil solitude of secluded havens? Understanding your travel style will help you curate an experience that aligns with your preferences.

If you thrive on spontaneity, leave room for unplanned detours, serendipitous encounters, and the thrill of embracing the unknown. Conversely, if you prefer a structured approach, carefully plan your itinerary, ensuring you don't miss out on must-see attractions and cultural experiences.

A Personalized Journey Awaits

Your travel goals should be as unique as you are. Don't feel confined by conventional travel trends or societal expectations. Allow your individuality to shine through, crafting an itinerary that reflects your passions and desires.

Whether it's immersing yourself in the vibrant arts scene of a European metropolis, embarking on a wildlife safari through the African savanna, or exploring the ancient temples of Southeast Asia, let your heart guide you towards experiences that ignite your soul.

A Journey of Discovery

The world is a vast and diverse tapestry of destinations, each offering its own unique charm and allure. Let's embark on a journey of discovery, exploring some of the most captivating destinations that await your exploration.

Cultural Immersion: Delving into the Heart of Local Traditions For those seeking cultural immersion, consider venturing into the vibrant cities of India,

Hindu traditions, savor the aromatic flavors of traditional cuisine, and witness the mesmerizing spectacle of Bollywood. Or, journey to the ancient land of Japan, where you can experience the serenity of Zen gardens, witness the graceful movements of Geishas, and indulge in the culinary artistry of sushi and tempura.

DECIDING WHERE TO GO

The world of literature is a vast and captivating realm, offering a myriad of destinations to explore through the written word. Whether you seek historical epics, captivating romances, or fantastical journeys, choosing the right book can transport you to diverse worlds and enrich your understanding of different cultures and perspectives.

Before embarking on your literary adventure, delve into your personal reading preferences. What genres ignite your curiosity? Do you seek the thrill of adventure, the solace of romance, or the intellectual stimulation of historical fiction?

Consider your favorite authors, the types of stories that resonate with you, and the emotions you hope to evoke through your reading experience. Let your literary passions guide you, seeking out books that promise to transport you to captivating destinations.

The world of literature offers a kaleidoscope of genres, each catering to diverse tastes and interests. Delve into the realm of historical fiction, where you can immerse yourself in the grandeur of ancient civilizations, witness pivotal moments in history, and experience the lives of iconic figures.

Embrace the thrill of fantasy literature, where you can venture into fantastical worlds, encounter mythical creatures, and embark on epic quests. If romance is your quest, seek out captivating love stories that will sweep you off your feet, transport you to far-off lands, and evoke emotions that linger long after the final page.

Embracing Your Pace and Rhythm

Characters, and thought-provoking themes. Are you a voracious reader, eager to devour books at an accelerated pace, or do you prefer to savor each chapter, immersing yourself in the intricacies of the narrative? Understanding your reading style will help you select books that align with your preference.

If you thrive on fast-paced plots and cliffhangers, seek out page-turners that will keep you on the edge of your seat. Conversely, if you prefer a more leisurely reading experience, choose books with rich descriptions, intricate characters, and thought-provoking themes.

A Personalized Adventure Awaits

Your literary journey should be as unique as you are. Don't feel confined by conventional reading lists or expectations. Allow your individuality to shine through, selecting books that resonate with your passions and interests.

Whether it's immersing yourself in the world of Jane Austen's Regency England, embarking on a thrilling adventure with Sherlock Holmes, or exploring the dystopian future envisioned by George Orwell, let your literary curiosity guide you towards books that will enrich your imagination and broaden your horizons.

The world of literature offers a vast array of captivating destinations, each transporting you to a different time, place, and culture. Let's embark on a journey of discovery, exploring some of the most enchanting literary destinations that await your literary exploration.

Delving into the Annals of Time

For those seeking historical adventures, consider embarking on a journey through the ancient world with

"The Odyssey" by Homer, where you can follow the epic tale of Odysseus as he battles mythical creatures and navigates treacherous seas to return home.

Or, venture into the tumultuous era of the French Revolution with "Les Misérables" by Victor Hugo, where you can witness the struggles and triumphs of Jean Valjean amidst social upheaval and political turmoil.

Escaping into Worlds of Magic and Wonder

Embrace the magic of fantasy literature by immersing yourself in the enchanting world of "The Lord of the Rings" by J.R.R. Tolkien, where you can join hobbits, elves, dwarves, and other fantastical creatures as they embark on a quest to destroy the One Ring and save Middle-earth.

Venture into the fantastical realm of "Narnia" with C.S. Lewis's "The Chronicles of Narnia" series, where you can discover talking animals, mythical creatures, and a land where magic reigns supreme.

For those seeking romantic escapades, embark on a journey of love and self-discovery with Jane Austen's "Pride and Prejudice," where you can witness the witty banter and social intricacies of 19th-century England as Elizabeth Bennet and Mr. Darcy navigate their feelings for one another.

Or, immerse yourself in the timeless love story of "The Thorn Birds" by Colleen McCullough, where you can witness the passionate love affair between Meggie Cleary and Ralph de Bricassart, set against the backdrop of the Australian outback.

Embracing Your Unique Passion

As you explore these enchanting literary destinations, remember that your literary journey should be a reflection of your unique passions and interests. Whether you seek historical adventures, fantasy realms, and romantic escapades.

RESEARCHING YOUR LOCATION

Every location, whether bustling metropolis or tranquil countryside retreat, holds a unique tapestry of history, culture, and hidden gems waiting to be discovered. Ebooks, with their portability and vast array of titles, offer an invaluable tool for researching your location and enriching your understanding of its intricacies.

Ebooks provide a wealth of information on the historical context of your location, allowing you to trace its evolution from its earliest beginnings to the present day. Immerse yourself in captivating narratives that chronicle pivotal moments, influential figures, and the social and cultural transformations that shaped your surroundings.

Unveiling the Cultural Tapestry

Gain insights into the cultural nuances of your location through eBooks that explore its traditions, customs, art, music, and cuisine. Delve into the works of local authors, folklorists, and anthropologists to uncover the stories, beliefs, and practices that define the cultural identity of your area.

Step beyond the well-trodden tourist trails and uncover the hidden gems that make your location truly special. Ebooks can serve as your guide to lesser-known attractions, local haunts, and offbeat destinations that offer a glimpse into the authentic character of your surroundings..

Making the Most of Where You Call Home

The world is a vast and diverse place, filled with countless unique locations. Each one has a story to tell, a history to explore, and a culture to discover. Whether you're a lifelong resident or a recent transplant, taking the time to learn more about your location can be an enriching and rewarding experience.

Benefits of Location Research

There are many benefits to researching your location. By understanding the place you call home, you can:

Gain a deeper appreciation for your surroundings.

Understand the history and culture of your community.

Discover hidden gems and off-the-beaten-path destinations.

Connect with your neighbors and fellow residents. Become a more informed and engaged citizen.

In addition, location research can also be a valuable tool for personal growth and development. By learning about the social, economic, and environmental factors that shape your community, you can gain a better understanding of the world around you and your place in it.

Getting Started with Location Research

The first step in researching your location is to simply start exploring. Take some time to walk or drive around your neighborhood, visit local parks and landmarks, and talk to your neighbors. You can also find a wealth of information online and at your local library.

Here are a few tips for conducting effective location research:

Be specific about your research goals. What do you want to learn about your location? Once you know your goals, you can narrow down your research and focus on the most relevant information.

Use a variety of sources. Don't rely on just one source of information. Consult a variety of sources, such as books, articles, websites, and maps, to get a well-rounded view of your location.

Be critical of the information you find. Not all information is reliable. Evaluate the information you find before you use it. Consider the source, the date of publication, and the author's credentials.

Share your findings with others. Once you've learned something about your location, share it with others. This can help to educate others about your community and make a difference.

Tools for Location Research

In addition to traditional research methods, there are a number of digital tools that can be helpful for location research. These tools can help you to:

Map your location and identify points of interest. Access historical data and demographic information. Connect with local businesses and organizations.

Find and share community events. Learn about local environmental issues.

CHAPTER 3- Travel

SETTING A TRAVEL BUDGET

Traveling can be an expensive endeavor, but it doesn't have to be. By setting a travel budget, you can make sure you can afford your dream trip without breaking the bank.

The first step to setting a travel budget is to determine your travel goals. What do you want to get out of your trip? Do you want to relax on a beach, explore a new city, or experience a new culture? Once you know your goals, you can start to narrow down your options and figure out how much you'll need to spend.

When setting your budget, be sure to factor in all of your travel expenses, including transportation, accommodation, food, activities, and souvenirs. You can also add in a contingency fund for unexpected expenses. A good rule of thumb is to allocate 50% of your budget for transportation, 30% for accommodation, and 20% for other expenses.

Research Your Destination

Once you have a general idea of how much you want to spend, you can start to research your destination. This will help you to get a better idea of the cost of things like transportation, accommodation, and activities. You can also find out if there are any discounts available for students, seniors, or military personnel.

If you want to save money on travel, it's important to book your flights and accommodations in advance. This will help you to get the best possible prices. You can also sign up for email alerts from airlines and hotels to be notified of sales and promotions.

Be Creative with Your Accommodations

There are a number of ways to save money on accommodations, such as staying in hostels, camping, or renting an apartment. You can also consider staying outside of the city center, where prices are typically lower.

Be Flexible

If you're flexible with your travel dates, you can save money by traveling during the off-season. You can also consider flying into a smaller airport or driving to your destination.

There are a number of travel budget apps that can help you track your spending and stay on budget. These apps can also help you set realistic goals and track your progress.

Here are some additional tips for setting a travel budget:

1. Create a spreadsheet or use a budgeting app to track your expenses.
2. Set aside money for travel each month.
3. Consider using a rewards credit card to earn points on travel expenses.
4. Look for deals and discounts on travel websites and social media.
5. Don't be afraid to negotiate with hotels and other vendors.

CHAPTER 8

PLAN YOUR ITINERARY

Planning your itinerary can be an exciting and daunting task. It can be overwhelming to try to decide where to go, what to do, and how to fit it all in. But with a little planning, you can create an itinerary that is perfect for you.

An itinerary is a detailed plan of your trip. It includes your destinations, activities, and transportation arrangements. A well-planned itinerary can help you make the most of your time and avoid problems.

There are many benefits to planning your itinerary. Here are a few:

1. It helps you make the most of your time. By planning your itinerary in advance, you can make sure you don't miss out on any of the things you want to see and do.
2. It helps you avoid problems. By planning your transportation and activities in advance, you can avoid any last-minute hassles.
3. It helps you stay on budget. By knowing what you're going to spend on your trip, you can avoid any surprises.
4. It helps you relax and enjoy your trip. When you know what you're going to do, you can relax and enjoy your trip without worrying about planning.

There are a few steps you can take to plan your itinerary:

1. Determine your travel goals. What do you want to get out of your trip? Do you want to relax on a beach, explore a new city, or experience a new culture?

2. Research your destination. Once you know your goals, you can start to research your destination. This includes learning about the history, culture, and attractions of the place you're visiting.

3. Create a list of potential activities. Once you know about your destination, you can start to create a list of potential activities. This could include visiting museums, going on tours, hiking, swimming, or simply relaxing on the beach.

4. Prioritize your activities. Once you have a list of potential activities, you need to prioritize them. This will help you decide which activities are most important to you and make sure you don't miss out on them.

5. Book your travel. Once you have a general idea of your itinerary, you can start to book your

travel. This includes booking your flights, accommodations, and activities.

1. Create a daily schedule. Once you have your travel booked, you can create a daily schedule. This will help you make the most of your time and avoid any last-minute hassles.

Here are a few tips for planning your itinerary:

1. Be realistic. Don't try to cram too much into your itinerary. You'll need time to relax and enjoy your trip.
2. Don't be afraid to be flexible. Things don't always go according to plan, so be prepared to be flexible.
3. Leave some time for free time. Don't schedule every minute of your trip. Leave some time for free time to explore and relax.
4. Use a travel planner. There are a number of travel planners available that can help you plan your itinerary.
5. Ask for help. If you're feeling overwhelmed, ask a friend or family member for help.

Creating a daily schedule

Once you have your travel booked, you can start to create a daily schedule. This will help you make the most of your time and avoid any last-minute hassles. Here are a few tips for creating a daily schedule:

Start with your must-do activities. Make sure you schedule your must-do activities first. This will help you make sure you don't miss out on them.

Allow enough time for travel. Be sure to factor in travel time when creating your schedule. You don't want to spend your whole day getting from one place to another.

Schedule breaks. Take some time each day to relax and recharge.

Be flexible. Things don't always go according to plan, so be prepared to be flexible.

CRAFTING YOUR PERFECT ITINERARY

Traveling can be an enriching and rewarding experience, allowing you to explore new cultures, broaden your horizons, and create memories that will last a lifetime. However, planning a trip can be a daunting task, especially if you're trying to fit everything you want to do into a limited amount of time. That's where creating a well-crafted itinerary comes in.

An itinerary is a detailed plan of your trip that outlines your destinations, activities, transportation arrangements, and accommodation. It's your roadmap to a successful and enjoyable travel experience.

Setting the Stage

Before diving into the nitty-gritty of planning your itinerary, it's essential to establish a clear framework for your trip. This involves defining your travel goals, researching your destination, and setting a realistic budget.

What do you hope to achieve on your trip? Are you seeking relaxation on a secluded beach, an adrenaline- pumping adventure, or a cultural immersion into a new world? Clearly defined goals will guide your itinerary choices and ensure your trip aligns with your aspirations.

Familiarize yourself with your chosen destination's history, culture, attractions, and transportation options. This will help you make informed decisions about what to see and do, and how to navigate the area effectively.

Determine your overall budget for the trip, including transportation, accommodation, activities, meals, and any additional expenses. This will help you prioritize activities and make financially sound decisions.

With the foundation laid, it's time to craft your itinerary, the backbone of your travel adventure.

Prioritize Your Must-Do Activities

Identify the activities that are essential to your travel experience, whether it's visiting iconic landmarks, exploring hidden gems, or engaging in unique cultural experiences. Prioritize these activities to ensure they are included in your itinerary.

Factor in travel time between destinations and activities to avoid rushing and ensure a smooth flow throughout your trip. Plan transportation options and accommodation that align with your itinerary.

While it's tempting to pack your itinerary with exciting activities, don't forget to schedule downtime for relaxation and rejuvenation. This will prevent burnout and allow you to fully appreciate each experience.

Embrace Flexibility

Unforeseen events can happen, so be prepared to adapt your itinerary if necessary. Embrace spontaneity and allow for unexpected discoveries along the way.

Numerous tools and resources can aid in crafting Read travel blogs and participate in travel forums for insider tips, recommendations, and real-life experiences from fellow travelers.

Travel Guides and Maps

Consult travel guides and maps to gain a deeper understanding of your destination, including local transportation routes and hidden gems off the beaten path.

CHAPTER 4- ACCOMODATION

BOOKING FLIGHTS AND ACCOMMODATION

Whether you are a seasoned traveler or planning your first trip abroad, this chapter will provide you with the essential information and tips to make the process as smooth and stress-free as possible.

Choosing Your Airline

The first step in booking your flights is to choose an airline. There are a number of factors to consider when making your decision, such as price, schedule, amenities, and safety record.

Once you have chosen an airline, you can start searching for flights. There are a number of websites and apps that can help you with this.

When searching for flights, be sure to enter your travel dates, departure and arrival airports, and the number of passengers. You can also filter your results by price, airline, layover time, and other factors.

Once you have found the flights you want, you can book them directly with the airline or through a travel agency. Be sure to read the airline's terms and conditions carefully before booking.

Tips for Booking Flights

- Book your flights in advance, especially if you are traveling during peak season.
- Consider flying on a budget airline.
- Be flexible with your travel dates.
- Sign up for email alerts from airlines to be notified of sales and promotions.
- Look for packages that include flights and accommodation.

Choosing Your Accommodation

The type of accommodation you choose will depend on your budget, travel style, and personal preferences. There are a variety of options available, including hotels, hostels, Airbnb rentals, and vacation rentals.

Once you have chosen the type of accommodation you want, you can start searching for a place to stay. There are a number of websites and apps that can help you with this.

When searching for accommodation, be sure to enter your travel dates, the number of guests, and your desired location. You can also filter your results by price, amenities, and type of accommodation.

Once you have found the accommodation you want, you can book it directly with the property or through a travel agency. Be sure to read the property's terms and conditions carefully before booking.

LODGING AND ACCOMMODATIONS

Lodging and accommodations are an essential part of the travel experience. Whether you're on a business trip or a family vacation, you'll need a place to stay.

There are many different types of lodging and accommodations available, so it can be difficult to know where to start. This chapter will provide an overview of the different types of lodging and accommodations available, as well as some tips for choosing the right option for your needs.

Types of Lodging and Accommodations

There are many different types of lodging and accommodations available, but they can be broadly divided into two categories: commercial and non- commercial.

- Commercial lodging is operated for profit and includes hotels, motels, resorts, va car rentals,and bed and breakfasts. Commercial lodging typically offers a variety of amenities and services, such as meals, laundry, and recreational activities.
- Non-commercial lodging is not operated for profit and includes hostels, camping grounds, and vacation rentals. Non-commercial lodging typically offers fewer amenities and services than commercial lodging, but it is often more affordable.

Hotels

Hotels are the most common type of commercial lodging. They offer a variety of room types and amenities, and they typically have a restaurant, bar, and pool. Hotels are usually classified by star rating, with five-star hotels being the most luxurious and one-star hotels being the most basic.

Motels

Motels are similar to hotels, but they are typically located along highways and are designed for motorists. Motels typically have fewer amenities than hotels, and they may not have a restaurant or bar.

Resorts

Resorts are typically located in scenic locations and offer a variety of amenities and activities, such as golf courses, tennis courts, and swimming pools. Resorts are often all-inclusive, which means that meals and activities are included in the price of the room.

Vacation Rentals

Vacation rentals are a popular option for families and groups. They offer more space and privacy than hotels, and they are often more affordable. Vacation rentals can be found in a variety of locations, in

Including houses, apartments, and condos. Bed and Breakfasts

Bed and breakfasts (B&Bs) are small inns that offer a home-like atmosphere. B&Bs typically have a breakfast to guests.

Hostels

Hostels are a budget-friendly option for backpackers and other travelers. Hostels offer dormitory-style accommodations, and they may also have private rooms. Hostels typically have a communal kitchen and lounge area.

Camping Grounds

Camping grounds offer a variety of campsites for tents and RVs. Camping grounds may also have amenities such as showers, restrooms, and fire pits.

BUDGET

First thing to consider is your budget. Lodging and accommodations can range in price from very affordable to very expensive. It is important to determine how much you are willing to spend on lodging before you start your search.

Needs

Think about your needs in terms of the type of accommodation you need. If you are traveling with a family, you will need a different type of accommodation than if you are traveling alone. Consider the size of the accommodation, the number of amenities, and the location.

Preferences

Finally, consider your preferences. Do you prefer a quiet, relaxing atmosphere? Or do you prefer a lively, social atmosphere? Do you want to be in the heart of the city or in a more remote location?

HOTELS AND OTHER OPTION

Hostels cater to budget-conscious travelers, offering dormitory-style accommodations with shared bathrooms and common areas. Hostels provide a social and communal atmosphere, making them ideal for solo travelers seeking to meet new people and experience local culture. Many hostels offer additional services, such as organized activities, tours, and communal kitchens.

Embracing the Outdoors

Camping grounds offer a rustic and immersive experience for nature lovers and outdoor enthusiasts. They provide campsites suitable for tents, trailers, or RVs, allowing you to connect with nature and enjoy the tranquility of the outdoors. Camping grounds may offer amenities such as showers, restrooms, fire pits, and picnic tables.

Resorts

Resorts are designed for relaxation and pampering, offering a world of amenities and activities within their premises. They cater to those seeking an all-inclusive experience, providing meals, entertainment, and recreational activities, such as golf, swimming, and spa treatments. Resorts are often located in scenic destinations, offering a tranquil escape from the hustle and bustle of everyday life.

FINDING DEALS AND DISCOUNTS

In the world of travel, saving money is an art form. Whether you're a seasoned traveler or a budget- conscious adventurer, finding deals and discounts can make your travel dreams a reality. This chapter will equip you with the essential strategies and techniques to uncover hidden savings, maximize your travel budget, and embark on unforgettable journeys without breaking the bank.

Utilize Travel Planning Websites and Apps

Embrace the power of technology to streamline your deal-hunting process. Travel planning websites and apps like Google Flights, Kayak, and Skyscanner offer comprehensive search and comparison tools, allowing you to compare prices across multiple airlines and accommodation providers. These platforms often feature price alerts, notifying you when prices drop for your desired destinations.

Delve into the world of specialized discount travel websites and aggregators. Platforms like Groupon, Travelzoo, and LivingSocial curate a selection of deals and discounts on flights, hotels, activities, and more. These sites often negotiate exclusive deals directly with travel providers, offering significant savings to savvy travelers.

Enroll in loyalty programs offered by airlines, hotels, and car rental companies. These programs often reward frequent travelers with points, miles, or credits that can be redeemed for discounts or even free travel. Additionally, consider membership perks offered by credit cards, such as travel insurance, cashback rewards, and airport lounge access.

Embrace Off-Season Travel and Shoulder Seasons

Travel during off-season periods, typically during the spring or fall shoulder seasons, to take advantage of lower prices and fewer crowds. Popular tourist destinations often offer significant discounts during these periods, allowing you to experience the same attractions without the hassle and expense of peak season travel.

Expand your accommodation options beyond traditional hotels. Explore hostels, vacation rentals, and homestays, which often offer more affordable and unique accommodation experiences. These options provide opportunities to immerse yourself in local communities and connect with fellow travelers.

Seek Out Free or Discounted Activities

Research free or discounted activities in your destination city. Many cities offer a variety of free attractions, such as museums, parks, and cultural events. Additionally, look for discount passes or coupons for popular attractions and activities.

If you're a student or senior, don't overlook the potential for student or senior discounts. Many airlines, hotels, and tourist attractions offer reduced rates for these demographics.

Follow Travel Bloggers and Social Media Groups

Stay updated on the latest travel deals and promotions by following travel bloggers and social media groups dedicated to travel deals and discounts. These sources often share insider tips, promo codes, and exclusive deals that you might not find elsewhere.

Subscribe to email alerts and newsletters from airlines, hotels, and travel websites. These alerts can notify you of upcoming sales, special offers, and last-minute deals and don't be afraid to negotiate prices, especially when booking accommodation or activities. Sometimes, simply asking for a discount or a better deal can lead to significant savings.

CHAPTER 5- PACKING STRATEGIES

Packing for a trip can be a daunting task. There are so many things to think about, and it can be hard to know where to start. But with a little planning and organization, it can be a smooth and easy process.

In this chapter, we will discuss some packing strategies that will help you pack like a pro. We will cover:

- What to pack
- How to pack
- How to pack efficiently

What to pack

The first step to packing is to figure out what you need to pack. This will depend on the length of your trip, the destination, and the activities you will be doing.

Here is a general list of things to pack for a trip:

- Clothes
- Toiletries
- Medications
- Electronics

- Chargers
- Travel documents
- Snacks
- Entertainment

Once you have a general idea of what you need to pack, you can start to make a list. This will help you stay organized and make sure you don't forget anything important.

How to pack

There are a few different ways to pack your belongings. The best way for you will depend on your personal preferences and the type of luggage you are using.

Here are a few tips for packing:

- Use packing cubes. Packing cubes are a great way to keep your belongings organized and prevent them from shifting around in your luggage.
- Roll your clothes instead of folding them. Rolling your clothes can save space and help prevent wrinkles.

- Use compression bags for bulky items. Compression bags can help you save space by compressing bulky items like sweaters and jackets.
- Pack heavier items on the bottom of your luggage. This will help prevent your luggage from tipping over.
- Leave room for souvenirs. You don't want to pack your luggage so tightly that you don't have any room for souvenirs.

How to pack efficiently

Packing efficiently is all about making the most of the space in your luggage. Here are a few tips for packing efficiently:

- Use the right size luggage. Don't try to cram everything into a small suitcase if you need more space. Invest in a larger suitcase or bring a carry- on bag in addition to your checked luggage.
- Wear your bulkiest items. If you have any bulky items, like sweaters or jackets, wear them on the plane instead of packing them in your luggage.

- Pack shoes in shoe bags. Shoe bags will help protect your clothes from dirt and debris.
- Use empty spaces to your advantage. Stuff small items, like socks and underwear, into empty spaces in your shoes and bags.
- Take advantage of pockets. Use the pockets in your clothes and bags to pack small items.

By following these tips, you can pack like a pro and make your next trip a breeze.

LUGGAGE AND PACKING ESSENTIALS

Packing for a trip can be a daunting task, especially if you're prone to forgetting essentials or end up overpacking. A well-crafted packing checklist can be your savior, ensuring you have everything you need without weighing you down with unnecessary items.

Packing checklists offer numerous benefits:

- Organization and Efficiency: Checklists streamline the packing process, preventing last- minute scrambles and ensuring you don't neglect crucial items.
- Reduced Stress and Anxiety: Packing checklists alleviate the stress associated with forgetting essentials, promoting a sense of calm and preparedness.
- Tailored to Specific Trips: Checklists can be customized to suit the destination, duration of the trip, and planned activities, ensuring you pack appropriately.
- Reusable and Adaptable: Once created, checklists can be reused for future trips, with

minor adjustments based on the destination and itinerary.

Creating a Packing Checklist:

- Gather Information: Gather information about your trip, including the destination, duration, weather conditions, and planned activities.
- Categorize Essentials: Divide your packing list into categories, such as clothing, toiletries, electronics, travel documents, and miscellaneous items.
- List Essentials Within Categories: Within each category, list all the essential items you need, considering the trip's specifics.
- Consider Personal Preferences: Include items specific to your personal needs and preferences, such as comfort items, entertainment, or medications.
- Prioritize Items: Mark essential items as "high priority" to ensure they don't get overlooked.
- Customize for Solo or Group Travel: Tailor the checklist for solo or group travel, considering shared items and individual needs.

Tips for Effective Packing Checklists:

- Use a Checklist Template: Utilize readily available checklist templates or create a customized one using a spreadsheet or note- taking app.
- Incorporate Visuals: Add images or icons to items for easier identification, especially for non- English speakers or those with visual impairments.
- Digital Checklists: Opt for digital checklists that can be accessed on smartphones or tablets for easy reference during packing and throughout the trip.
- Print Checklists: Consider printing physical checklists for easy reference during packing and for cross-checking items while packing.
- Regular Reviews: Review and update your checklists before each trip, ensuring they align with the specific itinerary and destination.

CREATING PAKING CHECKLISTS

Packing for a trip can be a daunting task, especially if you're prone to forgetting essentials or end up over packing. A well-crafted packing checklist can be your savior, ensuring you have everything you need without weighing you down with unnecessary items.

Packing checklists offer numerous benefits:

- Organization and Efficiency: Checklists streamline the packing process, preventing last- minute scrambles and ensuring you don't neglect crucial items.
- Reduced Stress and Anxiety: Packing checklists alleviate the stress associated with forgetting essentials, promoting a sense of calm and preparedness.
- Tailored to Specific Trips: Checklists can be customized to suit the destination, duration of the trip, and planned activities, ensuring you pack appropriately.
- Reusable and Adaptable: Once created, checklists can be reused for future trips, with minor adjustments based on the destination and itinerary.

Creating a Packing Checklist:

- Gather Information: Gather information about your trip, including the destination, duration, weather conditions, and planned activities.
- Categorize Essentials: Divide your packing list into categories, such as clothing, toiletries, electronics, travel documents, and miscellaneous items.
- List Essentials Within Categories: Within each category, list all the essential items you need, considering the trip's specifics.
- Consider Personal Preferences: Include items specific to your personal needs and preferences, such as comfort items, entertainment, or medications.
- Prioritize Items: Mark essential items as "high priority" to ensure they don't get overlooked.
- Customize for Solo or Group Travel: Tailor the checklist for solo or group travel, considering shared items and individual needs.

MINIMIZING AND PACKING LIGHT

Traveling light is essential for a stress-free and enjoyable travel experience. It allows you to move freely, avoid baggage fees, and navigate with ease. Packing light also encourages you to be more mindful of your belongings and appreciate the essentials.

The Benefits of Packing Light:

- Reduced stress and hassle: Traveling with less luggage means less to worry about. You won't have to struggle with bulky suitcases, manage multiple bags, or deal with baggage claim delays.
- Ease of movement: Lighter luggage makes it easier to get around, especially in crowded areas or when using public transportation. You'll be able to navigate airports, train stations, and city streets with ease.
- Avoidance of baggage fees: Many airlines charge fees for checked luggage, which can add up quickly. Packing light allows you to avoid these fees and save money.
- Increased mindfulness: With fewer belongings, you'll be more mindful of what you bring and use. This can lead to a more intentional travel experience.

- Appreciation for the essentials: When you pack light, you'll find that you really only need a few essential items. This can help you appreciate the simple things in life.

Packing Light for Different Types of Trips

- Beach vacations: For beach vacations, pack lightweight, breathable clothing, swimwear, sunglasses, a hat, and sunscreen. You may also want to pack a light jacket or sweatshirt for cooler evenings.
- City trips: For city trips, pack comfortable shoes that you can walk in all day, versatile clothing that can be dressed up or down, and a good camera or smartphone.
- Hiking trips: For hiking trips, pack sturdy hiking boots, moisture-wicking clothing, a rain jacket, a hat, sunscreen, and plenty of water.
- Business trips: For business trips, pack professional attire, a laptop, chargers, and any other business essentials.

CHAPTER 6 - TRANSPORTATION KNOW-HOW

Transportation is an essential part of modern life, enabling people to travel for work, leisure, and personal fulfillment. With a variety of transportation options available, it can be overwhelming to navigate the different systems and choose the best mode of travel for your needs. This comprehensive guide will equip you with the knowledge and strategies to become a transportation savvy traveler.

Understanding the Different Modes of Transportation

- Air Travel: Air travel is the fastest mode of transportation, making it ideal for long-distance journeys. However, it can be expensive and may involve security checks, baggage restrictions, and delays.
- Rail Travel: Rail travel offers a comfortable and scenic way to travel, especially for medium- distance trips. It's generally more affordable

than air travel and can be less susceptible to weather disruptions.

- Road Travel: Road travel provides the most flexibility and freedom of movement, allowing you to explore at your own pace and stop whenever you like. It's also a cost-effective option for short-distance trips.
- Public Transportation: Public transportation, such as buses, subways, and trains, offers a convenient and affordable way to get around cities and urban areas. It's an eco-friendly choice that reduces congestion and pollution.
- Water Travel: Water travel can be a relaxing and enjoyable way to travel, especially for longer journeys. It's often more scenic than other modes of transportation and can be a great way to experience coastal regions.

Tips for Efficient and Enjoyable Travel

- Enhance your transportation experience with these helpful tips:
- Utilize technology: Use navigation apps, travel websites, and mobile ticketing to plan your

routes, book tickets, and access real-time travel information.

- Pack light: Minimize baggage to reduce hassle and save on baggage fees.
- Be prepared for delays: Allow extra time for unexpected delays, especially during peak travel times.
- Consider alternative routes: Explore alternative routes or modes of transportation to avoid congestion and delays.
- Embrace local transportation: Immerse yourself in the local culture by experiencing the city's public transportation system.
- Respect local customs: Be mindful of local customs and etiquette when using public transportation or interacting with transportation providers.**Additional Resources**

Transportation websites: Visit the websites of transportation providers, such as airlines, railways, and public transportation authorities, for schedules, fares, and route information.

Travel guides: Consult travel guides for specific information on transportation options, routes, and tips for navigating different transportation systems in various destinations.

Local transportation maps: Obtain maps of local transportation networks, including bus routes, subway lines, and train stations, to plan your journeys effectively.

Transportation apps: Download transportation apps that provide real-time updates on schedules, fares, and disruptions, as well as navigation assistance.

GETTING TO YOUR DESTINATION

The thrill of embarking on a journey, whether it's a short weekend getaway or an extended adventure across the globe, is an exhilarating experience. However, the process of reaching your destination can often be filled with complexities and uncertainties. This comprehensive guide will equip you with the knowledge and strategies to navigate the various stages of your journey, ensuring a smooth and stress-free travel experience.

Planning Your Route: The Art of Strategic Navigation

- Destination: Clearly define your starting point and your final destination, including any intermediate stops or layovers.

- Transportation Options: Research and select the most suitable modes of transportation for each segment of your journey. Consider factors such as distance, travel time, cost, and convenience.

- Route Selection: Utilize maps, navigation apps, and travel resources to identify the most efficient and scenic routes. Consider factors such as traffic congestion, road conditions, and weather patterns.

- Time Considerations: Factor in travel time, potential delays, and any time zone changes to ensure you arrive at your destination on schedule.

- Accommodation and Logistics: Plan your accommodation arrangements and any necessary logistics, such as visa requirements, currency exchange, and local transportation options.

- Gearing Up for Your Journey: Essential Preparations for a Smooth Travel Experience

Transportation hubs can be bustling and overwhelming environments. Navigate them with ease by following these tips:

- Arrive Early: Allow ample time for check-in, security procedures, and baggage check.
- Know Your Surroundings: Familiarize yourself with the layout of the transportation hub, including terminal locations, gate numbers, and passenger information screens.
- Follow Instructions: Pay attention to announcements, signage, and instructions provided by airport or station personnel.
- Seek Assistance: Don't hesitate to approach information desks or staff members for assistance with directions, luggage storage, or any other questions.
- Maintain Awareness: Stay alert to your surroundings and keep your belongings secure.
- Embarking on Your Journey: Embracing the Adventure

NAVIGATING LOCAL TRANSPORT

Exploring a new city or region often involves navigating its local transportation system. Whether it's bustling city streets, tranquil countryside roads, or winding mountain paths, understanding the local transport options can transform your travel experience. This comprehensive guide will equip you with the knowledge and strategies to confidently navigate local transport, ensuring a smooth and immersive exploration of your destination.

Understanding Local Transport Systems: A World of Options

- Public Transportation: Public transportation systems, such as buses, trains, subways, and trams, provide convenient and affordable travel options within cities and urban areas.
- Taxis and Ridesharing: Taxis and ridesharing services offer point-to-point transportation, providing flexibility and convenience, especially for short trips and late-night travel.
- Local Buses and Minivans: In smaller towns and rural areas, local buses and minivans often

provide the primary means of public transportation, connecting villages and communities.

- Cycling and Walking: Cycling and walking offer eco-friendly and healthy ways to explore cities and neighborhoods, allowing for a closer connection to the local environment.
- Water Taxis and Ferries: In coastal cities and regions, water taxis and ferries provide scenic and convenient transportation options, connecting islands, waterfront districts, and neighboring cities.

RENTING CARS AND RIDE-SHARING

When traveling to a new destination, exploring the area's attractions and hidden gems often requires reliable and convenient transportation. Renting a car or utilizing ride-sharing services offers travelers the freedom and flexibility to explore at their own pace, whether it's navigating bustling city streets, venturing into scenic countryside, or embarking on road trips across vast landscapes.

Renting Cars: Unleashing the Freedom of the Open Road

Renting a car provides travelers with the ultimate freedom and flexibility to explore their surroundings at their own pace. Whether you're seeking the convenience of city driving or the thrill of exploring remote areas, renting a car allows you to create your own itinerary and discover hidden gems off the beaten path.

Advantages of Renting a Car:

- Unparalleled Flexibility: Plan your own routes, stop whenever you like, and enjoy the freedom to explore at your own pace.
- Convenience and Comfort: Travel on your own schedule, avoid crowded public transportation, and enjoy the comfort of your own vehicle.
- Exploring Remote Areas: Access destinations that may not be easily accessible by public transportation, allowing you to venture into nature or discover hidden towns.

- Family-Friendly Option: Renting a car is ideal for families, providing ample space for luggage, personal belongings, and child seats.

Considerations for Renting a Car:

- Cost: Renting a car can be more expensive than public transportation or ride-sharing services.
- Parking: Factor in parking costs, especially in urban areas, and research parking options near your destination.
- Insurance: Ensure you have adequate insurance coverage for the rental car.
- Driving Conditions: Be aware of local traffic rules, road conditions, and weather patterns.

Ride-Sharing: Embracing Convenience and Comfort

Ride-sharing services have revolutionized urban transportation, providing convenient and affordable point-to-point travel within cities. With the tap of a button, you can hail a ride from your smartphone and enjoy a comfortable and hassle-free journey to your destination.

Advantages of Ride-Sharing:

- Convenience and Accessibility: Request a ride from anywhere within the service area and be picked up at your doorstep.
- Affordability: Ride-sharing services often offer competitive fares compared to taxis.
- Real-Time Tracking: Track your ride's location in real-time and know your estimated arrival time.
- Avoidance of Parking Hassles: Eliminate the need to find parking, especially in congested urban areas.

Considerations for Ride-Sharing:

- Availability: Ride-sharing services may be less readily available in remote areas or during peak travel times.
- Surge Pricing: Be aware of surge pricing during periods of high demand, which can increase fares significantly.
- Limited Luggage Capacity: Ride-sharing vehicles may have limited luggage space,

making them less suitable for travelers with bulky luggage.

- Connectivity: Ensure you have a stable internet connection to request and track your ride.
- Making an Informed Decision: Choosing Between Renting a Car and Ride-Sharing

The choice between renting a car and using ride-sharing services depends on your individual needs, preferences, and travel itinerary. Consider the following factors to make an informed decision:

- Purpose of Travel: If you're exploring a city and primarily need transportation for short trips, ride-sharing may be more convenient and cost- effective.
- Destination: If you're venturing into remote areas or prioritizing the freedom to explore at your own pace, renting a car may be more suitable.
- Travel Group: For families or groups with more than three passengers, renting a car may offer more comfort and space.

- Luggage: If you have significant luggage, renting a car provides ample space and flexibility for your belongings.
- Budget: Consider the overall cost of renting a car, including fuel, parking, and insurance, compared to the potential fares of ride-sharing services.

CHAPTER 7 - THINGS TO CONSIDER

Navigating the Lodging Landscape with Confidence Securing the ideal lodging is an integral part of crafting a fulfilling travel experience. Whether you're a seasoned adventurer or embarking on your first escapade, understanding the factors to consider when booking accommodations is crucial for a seamless and enjoyable journey.

Destination and Purpose

Your travel destination and the purpose of your trip will significantly influence your lodging choices. If you're seeking a tranquil retreat amidst nature, a secluded cabin or a cozy bed and breakfast might be ideal. For a bustling city adventure, a centrally located hotel or a vibrant hostel could be perfect. Consider proximity to attractions, transportation options, and the overall atmosphere of the area.

Budget and Amenities

Establish a clear budget before embarking on your lodging search. Hotel prices can vary dramatically based on location, star rating, and amenities. Determine the level of comfort and amenities you require, such as a private bathroom, air conditioning, or a fitness center. Prioritize the essentials and be flexible on non-essential amenities to fit your budget.

Travel Companions and Room Type

If you're traveling with a partner, family, or friends, consider the size and layout of the accommodation. Hotels offer a variety of room types, including single, double, twin, and suite options. Consider the privacy needs of each traveler and ensure the room can comfortably accommodate everyone.

Guest Reviews and Reputation

Rely on the wisdom of fellow travelers by reading online reviews. Check reputable travel websites and forums for honest feedback on the hotel's cleanliness, service, amenities, and overall atmosphere. Reviews can provide valuable insights into the hotel's true character and potential areas for concern.

Booking Platform and Cancellation Policy

Choose a reliable booking platform that offers secure payment options and transparent policies. Carefully review the cancellation policy to understand the terms and conditions for modifying or canceling your reservation. Consider booking directly with the hotel, as they may offer exclusive deals or personalized service.

Location and Accessibility

Consider the location of the hotel in relation to your desired activities and attractions. If you plan to explore the city on foot, proximity to public transportation or walkable attractions is essential. If you're driving, access to parking and proximity to highways may be important.

Special Needs and Preferences

If you have any special needs or preferences, such as accessibility accommodations, pet-friendly policies, or family-friendly amenities, ensure the hotel can cater to your requirements. Communicate your needs clearly to the hotel during the booking process to avoid any disappointments.

Additional Costs and Fees

In addition to the base room rate, be aware of any additional costs or fees that may apply, such as resort fees, parking charges, or city taxes. Understanding these additional costs will help you accurately budget for your stay.

Booking in Advance and Flexibility

For popular destinations or peak seasons, booking accommodations in advance is highly recommended. However, maintain some flexibility in your travel plans, as unforeseen circumstances may arise. Consider travel insurance to protect your investment in case of unexpected cancellations or trip disruptions.

Embrace Local Experiences and Recommendations

While hotel staff can provide valuable insights, don't hesitate to engage with locals or fellow travelers for recommendations on hidden gems, local attractions, and off-the-beaten-path experiences. Embrace the opportunity to immerse yourself in the local culture and discover unique experiences beyond the typical tourist trail.

REVIEWS AND RATINGS

The Power of Feedback In today's interconnected world, reviews and ratings have become an indispensable tool for travelers seeking informed decisions about their accommodations. Whether selecting a hotel, exploring a restaurant, or planning an excursion, reviews provide valuable insights into the experiences of fellow travelers, offering a glimpse into the quality and overall satisfaction of a particular establishment.

The Role of Review Platforms

Numerous online platforms have emerged as hubs for traveler reviews, each offering its unique features and perspectives. TripAdvisor, Google Reviews, and Yelp are among the most prominent platforms, boasting extensive databases of user-generated content. These platforms enable travelers to share their experiences, providing a wealth of information and opinions that can guide future travelers' decisions.

Understanding Review Types

Reviews can take various forms, ranging from detailed narratives to concise star ratings. While star ratings provide a quick overview of overall satisfaction, detailed narratives offer a deeper understanding of the reviewer's experience, highlighting specific aspects of the accommodation, such as cleanliness, service, amenities, and overall atmosphere.

Evaluating Review Credibility

As with any online content, it's crucial to exercise discernment when evaluating reviews. Consider the reviewer's profile, the number of reviews they have written, and the consistency of their feedback across different establishments. Look for reviews that provide specific examples and insights, rather than relying solely on general statements or emotional outbursts.

Balancing Positive and Negative Reviews

While positive reviews can undoubtedly influence your decision, don't overlook the value of negative reviews. Negative reviews can shed light on potential issues or areas for improvement, providing valuable information that might otherwise go unnoticed. Consider the frequency and consistency of negative reviews to gauge the severity of any potential problems.

Utilizing Reviews Effectively

To effectively utilize reviews, adopt a holistic approach. Read a variety of reviews from different sources, considering both positive and negative feedback. Seek out reviews that align with your travel style, preferences, and priorities. Pay attention to recurring themes and patterns in the reviews to identify consistent feedback.

Respecting Diverse Perspectives

Remember that reviews reflect individual perspectives and experiences. Travelers have varying expectations, preferences, and travel styles, and their reviews will inevitably reflect these differences. Approach reviews with an open mind, considering the reviewer's background and their unique set of circumstances.

Additional sources of information

Reviews provide valuable insights, don't limit your research to online platforms. Consult travel blogs, guidebooks, and recommendations from friends, family, or travel agents for a more comprehensive understanding of the accommodation and its overall reputation..

CUITURAL INSIGHTS

Deepening Your Connection with Local Cultures Traveling to a new destination offers an unparalleled opportunity to immerse yourself in a different culture, broaden your horizons, and gain a deeper appreciation for the world's diversity. However, truly understanding and appreciating a culture requires more than just sightseeing and ticking off attractions on a list. It's about embracing cultural insights, respecting local customs, and engaging with the people who make the destination unique.

Cultural Sensitivity and Respect

Before embarking on your journey, take the time to learn about the local culture, customs, and traditions. Familiarize yourself with greetings, etiquette, and any taboos that might exist. Show respect for local beliefs and practices, and avoid making assumptions or judgments based on your own cultural background.

Language and Communication

Learning a few basic phrases in the local language can go a long way in establishing connections with locals and enhancing your travel experience. Even a simple greeting or a polite request can demonstrate your willingness to engage and make an effort to communicate.

Embrace Local Cuisine

Indulge in the local cuisine and savor the flavors that define the region. Try traditional dishes, visit local markets, and engage with food vendors to learn about the ingredients and preparation methods

Immerse Yourself in Local Activities

Participate in local festivals, attend cultural performances, and engage in activities that reflect the region's traditions. Immerse yourself in the rhythm of daily life and observe how locals interact with their surroundings.

Seek Local Perspectives

Engage in conversations with locals, ask questions, and listen to their stories. Seek out their recommendations for hidden gems, local hangouts, and authentic experiences that go beyond the typical tourist trail

Respectful Interactions

Be mindful of local dress codes and customs. Dress appropriately for visits to religious sites or cultural institutions. Ask permission before taking photographs of people or sacred places

Responsible Tourism

Choose sustainable travel practices that minimize your impact on the environment and local communities. Support local businesses, patronize eco-friendly establishments, and respect natural spaces.

Cultural Exchange and Openness

Approach cultural encounters with an open mind and a willingness to learn. Be prepared to step outside your comfort zone and embrace new experiences, perspectives, and ways of life.

Cultural Appreciation and Understanding

As you interact with different cultures, develop an appreciation for their unique customs, traditions, and values. Recognize that cultural differences are not a sign of inferiority or superiority, but rather a reflection of the world's rich diversity.

Cultural Sensitivity and Adaptability

Be flexible and adaptable in your approach. Embrace unexpected situations as opportunities to learn and grow. Cultural sensitivity and adaptability are essential for a truly enriching travel experience.

RESEARCHING CULTURAL CUSTOMS

Navigating Cultural Landscapes with Understanding Venturing into a new destination opens doors to a world of cultural richness and diverse perspectives. However, to truly appreciate and immerse yourself in a different culture, it's essential to embark on your journey with an understanding of local customs and traditions. By conducting thorough research and preparing yourself for cultural encounters, you'll enhance your travel experience and forge meaningful connections with the people and places you encounter.

Embrace the Power of Knowledge

Before embarking on your adventure, dedicate time to researching the cultural customs of your destination. Familiarize yourself with local greetings, etiquette, and social norms. Understanding these nuances will help you avoid unintentional faux pas and foster positive interactions with locals.

Seek Reputable Sources

Utilize reliable sources to gather information about the culture. Consult travel guides, cultural websites, and embassy websites to gain insights into local customs, traditions, and beliefs. Engage with online communities and forums where travelers share their experiences and cultural learnings

A Bridge to Understanding

Even a few basic phrases in the local language can go a long way in bridging cultural gaps. Learn simple greetings, expressions of gratitude, and phrases related to common needs. Making an effort to communicate in the local tongue demonstrates your willingness to engage and respect the culture.

Observe and Learn

Upon your arrival, observe how locals interact with each other and their surroundings. Pay attention to nonverbal cues, gestures, and body language. These subtle observations can provide valuable insights into cultural norms and expectations.

Engage with Locals

Strike up conversations with locals, ask questions, and listen attentively to their stories. Seek their recommendations for authentic experiences that go beyond the typical tourist trail. Engage with local businesses and support their endeavors.

Be Respectful and Adaptable

Approach cultural encounters with an open mind and a willingness to learn. Be respectful of local customs, beliefs, and traditions. Embrace unexpected situations as opportunities to gain cultural insights and adapt your behavior accordingly.

Mindful Dress and Conduct

Familiarize yourself with local dress codes, particularly when visiting religious sites or cultural institutions. Dress appropriately to show respect for the culture and avoid unintentional offense.

Photography with Sensitivity

Always ask permission before taking photographs of people or sacred places. Be mindful of cultural sensitivities and avoid capturing images that may be considered disrespectful or intrusive.

Cultural Exchange and Openness

Embrace cultural exchange as an opportunity to learn and grow. Share your own cultural perspectives while being open to new experiences and ways of life. Engage in conversations that foster understanding and appreciation of cultural differences.

Cultural Sensitivity and Responsibility Choose sustainable travel practices that minimize your impact on the environment and local communities. Support local businesses, patronize eco-friendly establishments, and respect natural spaces.

CHAPTER 8
LANGUAGE AND COMMUNICATION

Navigating the World with Linguistic Confidence Language, the essence of human interaction, can be both a bridge and a barrier for travelers venturing into new destinations. While understanding the local language enhances the travel experience, the reality is that language barriers often arise. However, with the right strategies and a willingness to communicate, travelers can overcome these barriers and forge meaningful connections with people from diverse cultures.

Embrace Basic Phrases

Learning a few basic phrases in the local language can go a long way in establishing connections with locals. Even simple greetings, expressions of gratitude, and phrases related to common needs can demonstrate your willingness to engage and make an effort to communicate.

Utilize Translation Tools

Leverage language translation apps and dictionaries to bridge language gaps. These tools can provide real-time translation support for basic conversations and sign language assistance. While not a substitute for fluency, they can be helpful in navigating everyday situations.

Practice Nonverbal Communication

Nonverbal communication, including gestures, facial expressions, and body language, plays a significant role in cross-cultural interactions. Be mindful of your nonverbal cues and observe how locals communicate nonverbally. A smile, a nod, or a gesture of gratitude can convey understanding and respect.

Seek Assistance from Locals

Don't hesitate to seek assistance from locals who speak your language. Approach hotel staff, fellow travelers, or even friendly locals for help with directions, recommendations, or translations. Most people are happy to assist and appreciate your efforts to communicate.

Embrace the Challenge

View language barriers as opportunities for learning and growth. Embrace the challenge of communicating in a new language, even if you make mistakes. Locals will appreciate your effort and enjoy the interaction.

Understand Cultural Differences

Be aware of cultural differences in communication styles. In some cultures, directness is valued, while in others, indirectness is preferred. Observe local communication norms and adapt your approach accordingly.

Patience and Humor

Approach language barriers with patience and humor. Misunderstandings are to be expected, but a lighthearted attitude and a willingness to laugh can help overcome awkward situations and build rapport.

Embrace Technology

Utilize language learning apps and online resources to enhance your vocabulary and improve your pronunciation. Even a few hours of dedicated practice can make a significant difference in your ability to communicate effectively.

Seek Language Exchange Opportunities

Engage in language exchange programs or connect with locals who are interested in learning your language. These exchanges provide opportunities to practice your language skills and gain cultural insights in a natural setting.

Embrace the Journey

View language learning as an ongoing journey rather than a destination. Embrace the challenges, celebrate the progress, and enjoy the process of discovering a new language and culture.

CONNECTING WITH LOCALS

Travel offers an unparalleled opportunity to immerse yourself in diverse cultures, broaden your horizons, and connect with people from all walks of life. While sightseeing and ticking off attractions are important, the true essence of travel lies in forging meaningful connections with locals, gaining insights into their way of life, and creating lasting memories.

Venture Beyond Tourist Trails

Step away from the well-trodden tourist paths and venture into neighborhoods where locals live, work, and gather. Explore local markets, patronize family-owned restaurants, and visit parks and community centers frequented by residents.

Engage in Casual Conversations

Strike up conversations with locals in everyday settings, such as coffee shops, grocery stores, or while waiting in line. Initiate simple exchanges about the weather, local recommendations, or their daily routines.

Seek Local Perspectives

Ask locals for their recommendations on hidden gems, authentic experiences, and places that truly reflect the local culture. Engage in conversations about their traditions, challenges, and hopes for the future.

Participate in Local Events

Attend cultural events, festivals, and community gatherings to immerse yourself in the local spirit. Observe how people interact, participate in activities, and appreciate the vibrant atmosphere.

Embrace Cultural Exchange

your own cultural perspectives, traditions, and experiences while being open to learning about theirs. Engage in respectful discussions that foster mutual understanding.

Volunteer Your Time

Offer your time and skills to local organizations or community projects. Volunteering provides an opportunity to connect with locals, contribute to their community, and gain a deeper understanding of their lives.

Support Local Businesses

Patronize local businesses, shops, and restaurants. Engage with the owners, inquire about their products or services, and show appreciation for their contribution to the community's identity.

Respectful Interactions

Be mindful of local customs, dress codes, and religious sensitivities. Approach interactions with respect, humility, and a willingness to learn from different perspectives.

Embrace Unexpected Encounters

Welcome serendipitous encounters and spontaneous conversations. These unplanned interactions often lead to the most genuine and memorable connections with locals.

Cultural Sensitivity and Adaptability

Be open to adapting your behavior and communication style to suit the local context. Observe cultural norms, show respect for local traditions, and approach interactions with an open mind and a willingness to embrace new experiences.

STAYING SAFE AND HEALTHY

Prioritizing Well-being for a Smooth and Enjoyable Journey

Venturing into new destinations and immersing oneself in diverse cultures is an enriching and rewarding experience. However, it's crucial to prioritize your safety and health throughout your travels to ensure a smooth and enjoyable journey. By taking proactive measures, staying informed, and adapting to new environments, you can minimize risks and safeguard your well-being while exploring the world.

Preparation and Planning

Before embarking on your travels, conduct thorough research on your destination, including its safety profile, cultural norms, and potential health risks. Familiarize yourself with common safety concerns, local laws, and any areas to avoid.

Destination-Specific Immunizations

Consult with a healthcare professional or travel clinic to determine if any vaccinations or medications are recommended for your destination. Ensure you are up- to-date on routine vaccinations, such as measles, mumps, and rubella (MMR).

Travel Insurance

Obtain travel insurance that covers medical expenses, trip cancellation or interruption, and emergency evacuation. Carefully review the policy details and ensure it meets your travel needs.

Personal Safety Measures Stay Alert and Aware Be mindful of your surroundings, especially in crowded areas or unfamiliar environments. Trust your instincts and avoid situations that make you feel uncomfortable. Protect Your Belongings Keep valuables secure, such as your passport, wallet, and travel documents. Consider using a money belt or a hidden pouch. Avoid carrying large amounts of cash and be cautious when using ATMs.

Communicate Your Itinerary Inform friends or family about your travel plans, including your itinerary, accommodation details, and emergency contact information. Check in with them regularly to keep them updated on your whereabouts.

Health and Wellness

Practice proper hand hygiene, especially before eating or after touching public surfaces. Use hand sanitizer when soap and water are not available.

Food and Water Safety Drink bottled or boiled water to avoid waterborne illnesses. Choose reputable restaurants and avoid street food that is not properly cooked or stored.

Stay Hydrated Drink plenty of fluids throughout the day to prevent dehydration, especially in hot or humid climates.

Rest and Recuperation Prioritize adequate sleep and rest to maintain your immune system and energy levels. Avoid overexertion, especially in extreme temperatures or high-altitude environments.

Adapting to New Environments

Cultural Awareness and Sensitivity Respect local customs, traditions, and religious beliefs. Dress modestly in accordance with local norms. Avoid making assumptions or generalizations about people based on their cultural background.

Environmental Awareness Be mindful of local environmental regulations and conservation efforts. Respect natural spaces and avoid damaging or disturbing wildlife.

Be open to learning about their culture and Respectful Interactions Engage with locals with respect and humility. Avoid making intrusive requests or taking photographs without permission. perspectives.

Seek Assistance When Needed

Don't Hesitate to Seek Help If you encounter any safety or health issues, don't hesitate to seek assistance from hotel staff, local authorities, or emergency services. Utilize your travel insurance if necessary.

COMMON HEALTH AND SAFETY ISSUES

Ensuring a Smooth and Worry-Free Travel Experience Venturing into new destinations and immersing oneself in diverse cultures is an enriching and rewarding experience. However, it's crucial to be aware of common health and safety concerns that may arise during travel. By understanding potential risks, taking proactive measures, and adapting to new environments, you can minimize health risks and safeguard your well-being while exploring the world.

Traveler's Diarrhea

Prevention:

Practice proper hand hygiene, especially before eating and after using the bathroom.

Avoid consuming tap water, unpasteurized milk or dairy products, and raw or undercooked food.

Consider taking over-the-counter probiotics or traveler's diarrhea medication as a preventive measure. **Treatment:**

- Replenish fluids and electrolytes with oral rehydration solutions or clear broths.
- Over-the-counter antidiarrheal medications can provide relief.
- Consult a healthcare professional if symptoms persist or worsen.

Altitude Sickness

Prevention:

- Acclimatize gradually to high altitudes by ascending slowly and taking rest days.
- Avoid strenuous activities immediately upon arrival at high altitudes.
- Stay hydrated and maintain a healthy diet

Symptoms:

- Headache
- Nausea
- Dizziness
- Fatigue
- Shortness of breath

Treatment:

- Descend to a lower altitude if symptoms worsen.

- Over-the-counter pain relievers may help alleviate headaches.
- Consult a healthcare professional if symptoms persist or become severe.

Mosquito-Borne Diseases

Prevention:

- Wear long-sleeved shirts and pants, especially during dusk and dawn when mosquitoes are most active.
- Apply insect repellent with DEET, picaridin, or IR3535 to exposed skin.
- Consider using mosquito nets or sleeping in air-conditioned accommodations.

Diseases:

- Malaria
- Dengue fever
- Zika virus
- Chikungunya virus Symptoms:
- Fever
- Headache
- Muscle aches

- Fatigue
- Rash

Treatment:

Consult a healthcare professional if you experience symptoms of mosquito-borne diseases.

Treatment depends on the specific disease and may include medications, rest, and supportive care.

Travel-Related Injuries

Prevention:

- Be aware of your surroundings and take caution when walking in unfamiliar areas.
- Avoid walking alone in poorly lit or deserted areas, especially at night.
- Wear comfortable and supportive shoes to prevent slips and falls.
- Store valuables securely and avoid displaying expensive items in public.

Treatment:

- Seek immediate medical attention for serious injuries.

- Minor injuries can be treated with over-the- counter pain relievers, cold compresses, and elevation.

Food Allergies and Sensitivities Prevention:

- Inform restaurants and accommodation providers about your food allergies or sensitivities beforehand.
- Carry a translation card for your allergies in the local language.
- Avoid consuming unfamiliar foods or ingredients if you have concerns.

Treatment:

- Antihistamines can help alleviate mild allergic reactions.
- In severe cases, seek immediate medical attention for anaphylactic reactions.

PRECAUTIONS RISKY AREAS

Venturing into Challenging Environments with Safety and Awareness .The allure of the unknown often draws travelers to explore remote, unconventional, or politically unstable destinations. While these journeys can offer unique experiences and cultural insights, they also present unique risks and challenges. By understanding the potential hazards, taking proactive measures, and exercising caution and preparedness, travelers can mitigate risks and navigate risky areas with greater safety and confidence.

Risk Assessment and Awareness

Before embarking on a journey to a risky area, conduct thorough research to assess the potential dangers and identify areas of concern. Consult travel advisories, news reports, and local experts to gain insights into the current security situation, political climate, and any ongoing conflicts or unrest.

Register with Your Embassy or Consulate Register your travel plans with your embassy or consulate upon arrival in your destination country. This will enable them to locate you in case of an emergency and provide assistance if needed. Keep their contact information readily available.

Communication Strategies

Maintain open communication lines with family or friends back home. Regularly update them on your whereabouts, itinerary, and any changes in your plans. Consider using a satellite phone or other communication devices that can operate in remote areas.

Secure Your Belongings

Protect your valuables and travel documents by using secure storage options, such as hotel safes or hidden pouches. Avoid carrying large amounts of cash and be cautious when using ATMs or exchanging currency.

Travel Companions and Local Guide

A local guide who can provide valuable insights and guidance. Avoid venturing into unfamiliar or dangerous areas alone, especially at night.

Transportation and Accommodation Choices Choose reputable transportation providers and opt for safe and secure accommodation options. Avoid traveling in overcrowded or unsafe public transportation. Research hotel security measures and consider staying in centrally located areas with visible security presence.

Cultural Sensitivity and Respect

Dress modestly and respectfully in accordance with local customs and traditions. Avoid drawing attention to yourself or displaying expensive items. Be mindful of local etiquette and avoid making assumptions or generalizations about people based on their cultural background.

Adaptability and Flexibility

Be prepared to adapt your itinerary and plans based on changing circumstances. Remain flexible and avoid rigid schedules that may put you at risk. Stay informed about local events, political developments, and potential safety concerns.

Seek Assistance When Needed

Don't hesitate to seek assistance from hotel staff, local authorities, or emergency services if you encounter any safety or security issues. Utilize your travel insurance if necessary.

Evacuation Plans and Preparedness Familiarize yourself with emergency evacuation procedures and designated safe areas in your accommodation and destination city. Keep emergency contact information readily available and have a backup plan in case of unexpected situations.

HANDLING INJURIES AND EMERGENCIES

Embracing Preparedness for Unforeseen CircumstanceS .Travel, with its exciting adventures and diverse experiences, can sometimes lead to unexpected situations, including injuries and emergencies. While these incidents can be stressful and overwhelming, maintaining a calm and composed demeanor is crucial for effective response and ensuring the well-being of yourself and others.

Personal Preparation and First Aid Knowledge Before embarking on your travels, consider taking a basic first aid course to equip yourself with essential skills for managing common injuries and emergencies. Familiarize yourself with basic wound care, CPR techniques, and emergency protocols.

Emergency Preparedness Kit

Pack a well-stocked emergency kit containing essential supplies for treating minor injuries, such as bandages, antiseptic wipes, pain relievers, and antihistamines.

Consider including additional items based on your destination and activities, such as insect repellent, sunscreen, or emergency blankets.

Remain Calm and Assess the Situation

In the event of an injury or emergency, it's crucial to remain calm and assess the situation objectively. Take a deep breath and gather your thoughts before taking action. Evaluate the severity of the injury or emergency and determine the necessary course of action.

Prioritize Safety

Ensure the safety of yourself and others involved. If there is any danger present, such as ongoing hazards or potential risks, prioritize removing yourself and others from the immediate danger zone.

Administer First Aid

If you have first aid training, apply your knowledge to provide initial treatment for any injuries. Follow basic first aid principles, such as controlling bleeding, applying pressure to wounds, and elevating injured limbs.

Seek Medical Attention

For serious injuries or emergencies that require professional medical attention, seek assistance immediately. Contact emergency services, local hospitals, or medical clinics. Provide clear details about the situation and the patient's condition.

Emotional Support and Reassurance

Offer emotional support and reassurance to the injured person or those involved in the emergency. Provide comfort, listen attentively, and offer words of encouragement.

Cultural Sensitivity and Communication

If dealing with locals or individuals from different cultural backgrounds, be mindful of cultural sensitivities and communication barriers. Seek assistance from translators or individuals familiar with the local language and customs.

Documentation and Reporting

Document the incident, including details of the injury or emergency, the location, and any witnesses. Report the incident to local authorities or relevant parties if necessary.

Seek Professional Support When Needed

If you or someone involved in the incident experiences emotional distress or trauma, seek professional support from counselors, therapists, or crisis hotlines.

CHAPTER 9 - MAKING MEMORIES

Beyond the Destination: Cultivating Enduring Recollections Travel is not merely about ticking off destinations on a map; it's about immersing oneself in new cultures, forging connections, and creating experiences that transform into cherished memories. While souvenirs and photographs can serve as tangible reminders, the essence of travel lies in the intangible moments, the emotions evoked, and the lessons learned.

1. Embrace Authenticity and Unplanned Moments: Step away from the meticulously planned itineraries and allow room for serendipity. Embrace unplanned moments, unexpected encounters, and detours that lead to hidden gems and authentic experiences. These spontaneous moments often lead to the most memorable and cherished recollections.

2. Engage with Locals and Cultures:

Seek out interactions with locals, immerse yourself in their daily lives, and engage with their culture. Share meals, learn a few phrases, and participate in local customs. These interactions create deeper connections and foster lasting memories.

3. Capture Moments, Not Just Images:

While photographs can capture a moment in time, true memories are often embedded in emotions, sounds, and smells. Journal your experiences, record ambient sounds, or collect mementos that evoke the essence of a place.

4. Challenge Your Comfort Zone:

Venture beyond your comfort zone and embrace new experiences, whether it's trying unfamiliar cuisines, participating in local activities, or engaging in conversations with people from diverse backgrounds. These challenges often lead to personal growth and unforgettable memories.

5. Reflect and Appreciate:

Take time to reflect on your experiences, appreciate the beauty around you, and savor the moments that touch your heart. Gratitude and mindfulness enhance the experience and transform fleeting moments into lasting memories.

6. Share Your Stories and Inspire Others:

Share your travel stories with friends and family, relive the experiences through storytelling, and inspire others to embark on their own journeys. Sharing enriches your memories and creates a ripple effect of exploration and discovery.

7. Preserve Your Memories:

Organize your photographs, journals, and mementos into a personalized travelogue or scrapbook. These tangible reminders will allow you to revisit your memories and relive the emotions of your journeys.

8. Embrace the Journey, Not Just the Destination: Recognize that travel is a continuous journey of learning, growth, and self-discovery. Embrace the process, the unexpected turns, and the lessons learned along the way. These experiences form the foundation of cherished memories.

9. Cultivate Gratitude and Appreciation:

Express gratitude for the opportunities to travel, the people you encounter, and the experiences that enrich your life. Gratitude enhances the journey and transforms fleeting moments into enduring memories.

10. Create a Legacy of Memories:

Share your passion for travel with others, encourage them to explore the world, and inspire them to create their own cherished travel memories. Your legacy lies not only in the destinations you've visited but also in the memories you've created and the inspiration you've sparked.

JOURNALING AND MEMORY KEEPING

Preserving the Tapestry of ExperiencesTravel is a tapestry of experiences, emotions, and lessons woven together to create enduring memories. While photographs capture moments in time, travel journaling allows us to delve deeper, capturing the essence of our journeys through words, sketches, and collected mementos. Whether you're a seasoned writer or a casual note-taker, travel journaling offers a profound way to preserve the rich tapestry of your adventures.

Embrace the Power of Words

Travel journaling provides a canvas for your thoughts, observations, and emotions. Capture the sights, sounds, smells, and tastes of your experiences. Describe the vibrant colors of a bustling market, the intoxicating aroma of local spices, or the soothing melody of traditional music.

Sketch the Essence of a Place

If you're artistically inclined, incorporate sketches into your journal. Capture the architectural details of a historic monument, the vibrant hues of a local marketplace, or the serene beauty of a natural landscape. Your sketches will serve as visual reminders of your experiences.

Collect Mementos and Ephemera

Gather mementos and ephemera that represent your journey. Collect ticket stubs, postcards, maps, or even local currency. These tangible reminders will add depth and dimension to your journal and evoke memories when revisited in the future.

Embrace Authenticity and Honesty

Your travel journal is a personal reflection, so let your authenticity shine through. Write freely and honestly about your experiences, thoughts, and emotions. Don't be afraid to share your vulnerabilities, insights, and personal growth.

Capture the Moments Beyond Images

Travel journaling is not just about capturing what you see; it's about capturing the emotions you feel. Describe how a particular moment made you feel, whether it was the awe-inspiring beauty of a natural wonder, the heartwarming connection with a local, or the profound realization about a different culture.

Embrace the Power of Lists and Notes

Incorporate lists to organize your thoughts, impressions, and recommendations. Create lists of must-try dishes, hidden gems, local phrases, or cultural etiquette tips. These lists will serve as a practical guide for future travelers and a valuable reminder of your own experiences.

Seek Inspiration from Fellow Travelers

Read travel journals and memoirs written by others to gain inspiration and new perspectives. Learn how other travelers have captured the essence of their journeys and incorporate their techniques into your own writing.

Make Journaling a Daily Ritual

Set aside time each day, preferably at the end of the day, to reflect on your experiences and write in your journal. Capture the fresh impressions and emotions while they are still vivid in your mind

Experiment with Different Formats

Travel journaling doesn't have to be confined to traditional writing. Experiment with different formats, such as poems, short stories, or even a combination of writing, sketches, and collages. Find a style that resonates with you and allows you to express yourself creatively.

Preserve Your Journal for Future Generations

Your travel journal is a valuable record of your personal growth, cultural encounters, and transformative experiences. Preserve it carefully, share it with loved ones, and consider passing it down to future generations as a legacy of your travels.

PHOTOGRAPHY TIPS FOR TRAVELERS

Preserving Memories Through the Art of PhotographyTravel offers an abundance of opportunities to capture stunning landscapes, vibrant cultures, and fleeting moments that transform into cherished memories. Photography, as a powerful medium of storytelling, allows us to preserve these experiences and share them with others. Whether you're a seasoned photographer or a novice with a smartphone, these essential tips will help you elevate your travel photography and capture the essence of your adventures.

Embrace the Golden and Blue Hours

The golden hour, the period shortly after sunrise and before sunset, and the blue hour, the period shortly after sunset and before sunrise, offer exceptional lighting conditions for photography. The soft, diffused light creates a captivating atmosphere and enhances the colors of your subjects.

Capture the Essence of a Place

Go beyond the typical touristy shots and seek out images that reflect the unique character and charm of a place. Photograph local markets, everyday scenes, and people going about their daily lives to capture the authentic spirit of the destination.

Master Composition and Framing

Pay attention to the composition of your images. Utilize the rule of thirds, leading lines, and other compositional techniques to create visually appealing and balanced frames. Use natural elements, such as trees, buildings, or archways, to frame your subjects.

Experiment with Different Perspectives

Don't limit yourself to eye-level shots. Get down low to capture unique perspectives, such as a child's eye view of a bustling market or an ant's-eye view of towering skyscrapers. Climb to vantage points to capture panoramic vistas or aerial shots.

Capture People in Their Element

Photograph people in their natural environments, engaging in their daily activities. Ask for permission before taking portraits and respect their privacy. Capture expressions, emotions, and interactions that tell stories without words.

Embrace Natural Light

Whenever possible, utilize natural light for its flattering and versatile nature. Avoid harsh midday sun and opt for softer morning or evening light. Diffuse harsh light by shooting through windows or under shade.

Master Exposure and White Balance

Understand the basics of exposure, such as aperture, shutter speed, and ISO, to control the brightness of your images. Adjust white balance to accurately capture the color temperature of the scene.

Edit with Intentionality

Enhance your images with editing software, but avoid over-editing. Use editing tools to adjust exposure, contrast, sharpness, and color balance subtly to bring out the best in your photos.

Capture Details and Texture

Zoom in on details and textures to add depth and interest to your images. Photograph close-ups of intricate architecture, weathered surfaces, or patterns in fabrics to showcase the beauty of the details.

Tell Stories with Your Images

Arrange your images in a sequence to create a narrative, guiding the viewer through your story. Each image should contribute to the overall message and evoke emotions in the viewer.